Bunnies

by Colleen Sexton

BELLWETHER MEDIA · MINNEAPOLIS, MN

Note to Librarians, Teachers, and Parents:

Blastoff! Readers are carefully developed by literacy experts and combine standards-based content with developmentally appropriate text.

Level 1 provides the most support through repetition of high-frequency words, light text, predictable sentence patterns, and strong visual support.

Level 2 offers early readers a bit more challenge through varied simple sentences, increased text load, and less repetition of high-frequency words.

Level 3 advances early-fluent readers toward fluency through increased text and concept load, less reliance on visuals, longer sentences, and more literary language.

Level 4 builds reading stamina by providing more text per page, increased use of punctuation, greater variation in sentence patterns, and increasingly challenging vocabulary.

Level 5 encourages children to move from "learning to read" to "reading to learn" by providing even more text, varied writing styles, and less familiar topics.

Whichever book is right for your reader, Blastoff! Readers are the perfect books to build confidence and encourage a love of reading that will last a lifetime!

This edition first published in 2008 by Bellwether Media.

No part of this publication may be reproduced in whole or in part without written permission of the publisher. For information regarding permission, write to Bellwether Media Inc., Attention: Permissions Department, Post Office Box 19349, Minneapolis, MN 55419.

Library of Congress Cataloging-in-Publication Data
Sexton, Colleen A., 1967–
  Bunnies / by Colleen Sexton.
    p. cm. – (Blastoff! Readers: Watch animals grow)
Summary: "A basic introduction to baby bunnies and how they grow. Simple text and full color photographs. Developed by literacy experts for students in kindergarten through third grade"–Provided by publisher.
  Includes bibliographical references and index.
  ISBN-13: 978-1-60014-166-9 (hardcover : alk. paper)
  ISBN-10: 1-60014-166-8 (hardcover : alk. paper)
  1. Rabbits–Growth–Juvenile literature. I. Title.

QL737.L32S39 2008
599.32–dc22   2007040271

Contents

These bunnies
were just born.
They have no
fur. Their eyes
are closed.

Bunnies sleep in a warm **nest**. Their fur grows. Soon they open their eyes.

Bunnies leave
the nest after
a few weeks.

Bunnies stay close to their mother. They drink her milk to grow strong and healthy.

Bunnies grow long teeth. Now bunnies can eat **greens**.

Bunnies grow
long ears.
They can hear
sounds from
far away.

Bunnies are busy.
They like to dig,
hide, and play.

Bunnies grow fast. Soon they have big feet and strong back legs.

Soon bunnies are
ready to live on
their own.

Glossary

greens—the leaves and stems of plants used for food; lettuce and spinach are examples of greens.

nest—a place where animals live and give birth to their young; bunny nests are made of fur from the mother bunny's body and grasses.

To Learn More

AT THE LIBRARY
Dunn, Judy. *The Little Rabbit*. New York: Random House, 2008.

Frankel, Laurie. *Funny Bunnies*. San Francisco, Calif.: Chronicle Books, 2004.

Magloff, Lisa. *Rabbit*. New York: DK Publishing, 2004.

ON THE WEB
Learning more about bunnies is as easy as 1, 2, 3.

1. Go to www.factsurfer.com

2. Enter "bunnies" into search box.

3. Click the "Surf" button and you will see a list of related web sites.

With factsurfer.com, finding more information is just a click away.

Index

The images in this book are reproduced through the courtesy of: Vladimir Popovic, front cover; Arco Images/Alamy, p. 5; Brook Johnson, p. 7; Morales/Age fotostock, p. 9; Arco/P.Wegner/agefotostock, p. 11; Sonderegger Christof/Age fotostock, p. 13; Greg Stott/Masterfile, p. 15; Morales/Age fotostock, p. 17; John Foster/Masterfile, p. 19; Renee Morris/Alamy, p. 21.